DANIEL O'CONNELL

SEAN McMAHON

MERCIER PRESS

107,472
£4-99

CONTENTS

CHRONOLOGY

1775	Daniel O'Connell born on 6 August; outbreak of American War of Independence
1789	Outbreak of French Revolution
1791-2	O'Connell and his brother Maurice at school at St Omer and Douai
1792–3	Relief Acts remove most Catholic disabilities
1793	Flight of the O'Connells to London after the execution of Louis XVI
1794	O'Connell at Lincoln's Inn
1795	Foundation of Orange Order
1796	O'Connell at King's Inns, Dublin
1798	O'Connell called to the Irish Bar; Irish rebellion
1801	Act of Union and O'Connell's public opposition to it
1802	O'Connell secretly marries his distant cousin Mary O'Connell
1803	Emmet's rising
1813	Trial of John Magee
1821	O'Connell presents a laurel wreath to George IV on the occasion of his coronation visit to Ireland
1823	Catholic Association
1824	Catholic rent
1826	Waterford election won by emancipation candidate

1828	O'Connell wins Clare by-election
1829	Catholic emancipation
1835	Lichfield House compact
1835-40	Thomas Drummond, reforming under-secretary, in office
1836	Death of Mary O'Connell
1837	Accession of Queen Victoria
1841	O'Connell Lord Mayor of Dublin
1843	Year of mass meetings; O'Connell arrested for conspiracy
1844	House of Lords frees O'Connell
1845-9	Potato famine
1846	O'Connell breaks with Young Ireland
1847	O'Connell dies in Genoa on 15 May

1

IVERAGH AND ST OMER

Daniel O'Connell was born on 6 August 1775, three-quarters of the way through what was called with some justice the Protestant century. The effects of the previous century's religious wars and the Catholic support for ungrateful Stuart kings had rendered the mass of the population leaderless and suspect and left most of the land of Ireland in Protestant hands. A series of penal measures enacted between 1695 and 1728 made it illegal for Catholics to keep weapons, to have their children educated abroad when schools were available at home, to buy land or inherit it from Protestants, to take out leases for longer than thirty-one years or to leave land to eldest sons, with all relict holdings to be subdivided equally among male heirs. An 'anti-popery' act of 1697 required all senior clergy to leave the country, and though other clergy were allowed to remain, their numbers were confined to one per parish and no clergy were allowed in from outside. All public offices were denied to Catholics, as were all of the learned professions except medicine.

The effects of these laws, which were general in Britain, was to confirm the ascendancy of the Protestant minority in Ireland and to render the majority population, which amounted to approximately two million, landless and disenfranchised – this last disability imposed in 1728. Most of the Catholics' natural leaders and the Jacobite army had been led into exile by Sarsfield after the unhonoured Treaty of Limerick, and so it was possible to say as the country settled down to inertia under a series of unlovely Hanoverian monarchs that 'the law does not suppose any such person to exist as an Irish Roman Catholic'.

While the British parliament was on the whole uncaring about Irish Catholics except insofar as they represented a security threat, the assembly that met in Chichester House was formally and instinctively anti-Catholic, as much from greed as from religious conviction. Conscious, perhaps, of the recency of their ennoblement, as contrasted with the peasants, who invariably and irritatingly claimed ancient lineage, their contempt for the underclass contained traces of unease, and their main purpose, apart from self-enrichment, was to deny the mass of the people the civil rights they insisted upon for themselves. The practices of the legal establishment, particularly the inept and partial judges who connived at the 'packing' of juries, meant that the instinctively litigious native Irish were usually at 'the mercy of the court'.

In fact the picture was not as universally bleak as some zealots might have wanted. The confessional legislation had fallen largely into abeyance by the 1730s; an unofficial toleration meant that Mass was said in private houses, barns and shelters generally without interference, priests in mufti and addressed as 'Mister' ministered as they could to their flocks and the various Irish colleges in Catholic Europe maintained their numbers. A suprisingly large number of Catholics grew rich in business, assuming a majority in such towns as Waterford, Cork and Limerick and tending to look to the continent rather than Britain for trading partners. As a character in Brian Friel's play *Translations* (1980) puts it, in a different

context: 'We feel closer to the warm Mediter-
ranean. We tend to overlook your island.' These
people evaded the travel restrictions and made sure
that their children, especially the sons, got the
education they felt was suitable for them in the
various continental seminaries that had been
established for recusants.

There were still some Catholic landlords, especially
in Connacht and Munster, who, by maintaining at
least a public show of loyalty to the British crown, had
a certain amount of autonomy. They could rely on the
remoteness of their holdings and the appalling
difficulties of travel to allow them a relatively untroubled
and prosperous existence. The story 'Connemara' in
Eyre Evans Crowe's collection *Today in Ireland* (1825)
gives a picture – only a little exaggerated – of the
almost medieval pattern of life west of the Shannon.
And it was in the remoteness of west Kerry that the
O'Connells, notably Maurice, Daniel O'Connell's
uncle, lived with some of the trappings and most of
the creature comforts of the old Gaelic aristocracy.

The year of O'Connell's birth coincided with the
outbreak of the successful American Revolutionary
War; three years later came the first Catholic Relief
Act; when he was seven Ireland achieved legislative

independence; and three weeks before his fourteenth birthday the fall of the Bastille was the signal that old regimes were not necessarily permanent. The Relief Act permitted Catholics to take longer leases than before and to leave property to a single heir; it also removed most of the restrictions affecting the Church and education. Acts of 1792 and 1793 allowed Catholics to practise law, to vote and to hold most civil offices; these measures were forced through by the government against the wishes of a majority of Protestants, however. All these factors were eventually to lead to the rise of modern democracy in Ireland, and Daniel O'Connell, the man largely responsible for the virtual re-creation of the Irish nation, was able to act as the liberator of his people as much because of these political and social changes as because of his undoubted personal genius. He was a man of his time as well as being *the* man of his time.

His early years were not unlike those of the degraded peasants whose champion he was to become. He was born at Carhen, near Cahirsiveen, in the Iveragh peninsula of west Kerry. His father, Morgan, was one of twenty-two children and, like his rich eldest brother, Maurice (universally known as 'Hunting Cap'), was a grazier, a merchant and, most significantly, a smuggler. O'Connell was from an early stage conscious of the living conditions of the large population of tenants-at-will, whose energies had to be devoted almost entirely to mere subsistence. The condition of 'the most degraded peasantry in Europe', driven to dreadful shifts simply to survive, especially in the years before the Great Famine of the mid-1840s, has been thoroughly documented. One small item will serve as an index of the condition: the prevalence of smoke blindness caused by the lack of chimneys in the mud huts that were the dwelling places of the very poor.

In fact, at the time of O'Connell's boyhood the peasants' diet of potatoes, milk, bacon and cheese, with fish (but rarely shellfish) for coastal dwellers, worked well. The strength of the *spailpíní* ('penny-a-day men') was proverbial and the pre-Famine visitors were impressed by the beauty of the women and the sense of gaiety that prevailed in spite of the appalling conditions. The peasants of Iveragh, endemic diseases like tuberculosis and typhoid aside, were perhaps healthier and better off materially than those in other parts of the country in that a remnant of the old sense of commonweal and chieftain-responsibility still existed. It is something of an exaggeration to suggest that Hunting Cap lived like a latter-day Red Hugh O'Donnell in his large house judiciously sited on the Kerry coast but he *was* an Irish Catholic landlord and as such was conscious of a moral duty towards his tenants that would never have occurred to the majority of Protestant – and often absentee – landlords.

One thing he shared with all Irish Catholics were the wearisome shifts and public mien that enabled the dispossessed to survive. He lived in a wary amity with his fellow, mostly Protestant, landlords, whose cellars he kept stocked and whose kitchens and dining rooms he supplied with exotic smuggled material. Like the other leading Catholics of the time, he was, in the words of one of them, Charles O'Conor (1710–91) of Belnagare, County Roscommon, a 'good Protestant in politics'. He utterly disapproved of the United Irishmen and indeed informed the government authorities of a possible French invasion at Bantry Bay in 1796. The godlessness of these Irish Jacobins appalled him as much as their threat to undo the slow work of a century of progress towards Catholic acceptability. Seven years later, in July 1803, his famous nephew was to stand as a militiaman against the insurgents in Robert Emmet's hopeless foray.

O'Connell had an even more famous uncle, a namesake of his, who had joined the French army when he was sixteen, in 1761, and who by 1788 was inspector-general of infantry and a count of the French court. He always had a soft spot for his nephew and it was he who persuaded Hunting Cap effectively to adopt the gifted youngster and got him out of several scrapes which the austere chatelain of Derrynane House would by no means countenance. It was he who, as if already aware that his nephew might be a personage of some significance beyond his native County Kerry, urged his rich, if frugal, brother to sponsor the boy's education in France.

The young Daniel spoke Irish, and, partly because of an ancient Irish practice of fostering and partly because the little house at Carhen had scant room for children, he was farmed out to one of his father's tenants. He did not return home until he was four, innocently admitting to his own father that he *had* eaten mutton before, recalling that his 'dad' had killed one of Morgan O'Connell's sheep. It was this early inculcation of modes of survival that caused O'Connell in later years not to seem to grieve over the near-disappearance of the Irish language. It played no part in his instinctively Benthamite crusade for the recovery of his people; and perhaps he was aware, as became clear in the later history of the Gaelic League, that the very act of revival of the Irish language was essentially revolutionary.

His acquaintance with the material in James Macpherson's *Ossian* (1763), noted in his diary in 1796, the year of the pasticheur's death, was hardly surprising since the carefully preserved oral lore, called *Fiannaíocht*, was a vital part of winter nights' entertainment in Gaeltacht areas like Iveragh. These tales of Oisín, his father Fionn and their warrior companions had survived nearly 2,000 years of troubled history and linguistic modification and were the Erse foundation for Macpherson's extremely popular romance.

Daniel O'Connell's utilitarianism in the matter of Irish has dismayed succeeding generations but for the people he was trying to rehabilitate it was in his view a luxury too far. He used Irish, again pragmatically, on political platforms where it was required and in the years of his 'Balmoral' seclusion in Derrynane in the decade before his death. His praise of 'the superior utility of the English tongue', recorded in W. J. O'Neill Daunt's *Personal Recollections* (1848), was not a policy statement but a postprandial conversational response. The same speech cited biblical authority for the view that diversity of speech was a curse 'imposed on mankind . . . at the building of Babel'. It also recognised that the language was 'connected with many recollections that twine around the hearts of Irishmen'. Besides, by the time the remarks were made, in 1833, the decision to have children abandon Irish had already been made by many hard-headed parents.

O'Connell's first school was essentially Derrynane, where Hunting Cap, his de facto guardian since 1780, had him tutored locally. Pleased with his academic reports, he sent him to a boarding school run by a Jesuit in Cork Harbour when he was fifteen. He continued to work hard, conscious of the debt he owed to his mentor and already aware, as several anecdotes indicate, of a kind of grand destiny awaiting him. Daniel and his brother Maurice, who was a year younger than him, were then sent to St Omer, fifty kilometres from Calais, arriving there in October

1791. The school had been chosen by their 'French' uncle but with France in the throes of revolution – and a godless revolution at that – he strongly urged Hunting Cap to wait until it was certain that the country was stable again. This sound advice was ignored and the boys were despatched to Liège, then in the Austrian Netherlands. As they were too old for entry to this school, they were taken in by the Franciscans in Louvain until Hunting Cap's intentions were made known, letters taking six weeks to arrive from Ireland.

St Omer was an English-speaking college that had been founded by Robert Parsons (1546–1610), an English Jesuit, two centuries before. Though it was now run by English seculars, the Jesuit system of the *Ratio Studiorum*, with its emphasis on a curriculum that would lead to excellence in the ancient classics, rhetoric and scholastic philosophy, still prevailed there. The boys learned French, studied English literature, and could engage in dancing, fencing and mathematics. They stayed there until August 1792, when a letter from Derrynane ordered them to proceed to Douai, another 'English' college a hundred kilometres away, where a higher syllabus was followed. The essential difference between its curriculum and that of a public school at home lay in its deliberate honing of forensic skills, by means of elocution, drama and oratory. For at least one serious student it was the very best vocational training.

The boys' schooldays were in fact to prove of relatively short duration because of the growing violence of the revolution in France. Not long after their arrival at Douai, the massacre by Marat of a thousand counter-revolutionaries in Paris prisons had shocked the governments of other European countries. The euphoria of *Quatorze Juillet* had been cruelly dispersed and the atmosphere of suspicion and terror continued to grow. Uncle Daniel, the royalist infantry general, fled to London that September and two months later, when Austria had invaded from the Netherlands, the schoolboys could hear the noise of the artillery. The move against Louis XVI and his family was gathering momentum and it was clear that Britain might at any moment declare war on revolutionary France.

By January 1793 the O'Connell brothers were on their way to England, their two-day journey to Calais made very frightening by mobs pummelling the coach. For safety's sake they wore the red, white and blue revolutionary favours but, once on the Dover packet, tossed them in the water. The effect of the French Revolution on Daniel both from what he had observed and from what he had heard was significant. The response of his teachers to the extremism and irreligion of the revolutionaries was predictable but it was his own sense of fear and his intolerance of anarchy that had the most profound effect on him. The day before the brothers reached Calais the king had been guillotined; the Terror that followed left the eighteen-year-old with a lifelong fear of violence and a distaste for the idea of armed uprising as a means of achieving political ends. He had seen how mob rule, the ultimate irrationality, could burgeon out of idealism, and his utter rejection of bloodshed was to be a source of great moral authority but ultimately the cause of impatience with O'Connell among the members of Young Ireland and a feeling that he had betrayed them.

107,472

2

LONDON, DUBLIN
AND THE OLD MUNSTER CIRCUIT

O'Connell was to spend three years in London, completing his legal education. He and Maurice attended a kind of school run by Chevalier Fagan, an Irishman who had been educated in France and was able to continue with minimal instruction and supervision and much setting of tasks the curriculum that the pupils had experienced at St Omer and Douai. This school placed the same emphasis as the other two had on rhetoric and logic – suitable subjects for a future lawyer, the career that Hunting Cap intended for his ward from the time when Sir Hercules Langrishe's measure of 1792 removed the ban on Catholics practising law. In January 1794, when he was still not yet nineteen, O'Connell enrolled at Lincoln's Inn as a first step on the rather informal path that would lead to a legal qualification. In March of that year Maurice ('Moss', in the usual Kerry style) left to join the army, with a commission to a lieutenancy, paid for by the long-suffering Hunting Cap. It was a generous gesture on the part of Hunting Cap, for Moss had got into many scrapes in London. He died of fever in San Domingo three years later.

O'Connell's London sojourn was characterised by near-penury. Hunting Cap was not generous and was insufficiently imaginative to appreciate that student life requires more money than that necessary for mere fees and subsistence. It would have been to the young student's advantage to have been attached to chambers but he lacked the money to pay the premium. He had, however, access to law libraries and plenty of leisure to build up a remarkable knowledge of precedent. His life in London was notably different from that in Derrynane, which he had not seen between 1791 and 1794, as Hunting Cap was deaf to subtly worded pleas to provide him with money for passage home. The uncle eventually relented and O'Connell spent the long vacation of 1795 in vigorous wild sports and country matters, which, though they dismayed Hunting Cap, were a salutary dip into Irishness again and stiffened the young man's resolve to return home as soon as possible. It seemed to him that King's Inns, grandly sited on Constitution Hill above the Liffey, had more relevance to his future career then either Lincoln's or Gray's Inn, to which he had had to transfer in May 1796.

Yet his metropolitan years were a significant part of his moral education. The capacity for learning is high between the ages of seventeen and twenty-one, and so is intellectual susceptibility. The spirit of the age was one of enquiry, challenge and concern for the rights of man. O'Connell, with his intellectual curiosity and sense of the grievances of his own countrymen, read and discussed the 'subversive' writings of Tom Paine (1737–1809), William Godwin (1756–1836) and Mary Wollstonecraft (1759–97). The effect was to make his views notably liberal, and he remained committed to the rights of women, the abolition of the slave trade and the removal of anti-Semitism, which was endemic.

At this time, too, O'Connell first considered deism as an alternative to the Catholicism in which he had been reared and educated. The belief in an original creator who was either asleep or who, having wound up the watch, felt no need for further maintenance seemed the best model for the free man in a world that seemed to show few signs of godliness. He remained a believer in the essential justice of that creator who would not punish genuine and informed doubt. He also regularly affirmed that sins against faith were more more grievous that those against morals. This may be read as a young man's convenience but it is a theologically sound attitude. Certainly as a tall, strong, handsome, brilliant young man of twenty with a musical voice and an effective wit he was unquestionably popular with women. Short of cash he may have been, but like Falstaff and Justice Shallow he had heard the chimes at midnight and definitely knew where the *bona robas* were. He fascinated his intellectually inclined landlady in Chiswick and, though there is no evidence for or against it, he probably had his moments as a bachelor boy at home in his not especially puritanical native county.

In later years his supposed sexual prowess became literally legendary. The assertion that Kerry and Dublin were full of his bastards was spread in hatred by his enemies and in compliment by his apotheosizing people, who assigned other mythic qualities to him. What is unquestionably true was his early and lasting love for his namesake, distant cousin and wife, Mary O'Connell (1778–1836), for whom he risked and indeed nearly lost his inheritance. She was the daughter of a Tralee doctor who had died in 1785, leaving her without the dowry that would have secured Hunting Cap's approval. They got engaged when he was twenty-five and she was three years younger, and as he later said, ' . . . she gave me thirty-four years of the purest happiness that man ever enjoyed'. Throughout his career until her death he relied on her greatly for advice, and her steadfast support helped him through the paternity suit that was brought in blackmail against him by Ellen Courtenay in 1831.

The Dublin he got to know in 1796 was buzzing with the excitement of a possible French invasion urged by the United Irishmen led by Wolfe Tone (1763–98), who had arrived in France on 1 February. Like all law students he found it judicious to join one of the civilian militias, the Lawyers' Artillery. Yet he was not unsympathetic to the ideals of Tone and Mc-Cracken. The free rein given to the Orangemen in Ulster and their murderous harassment of Catholics meant that, moderate as he was, he would naturally have shared some of the United Irishmen's beliefs. His membership of the corps was more than just cover, however: his experiences five years earlier had left him with a deep distrust of the French and his old abhorrence of revolution. He did not believe that the Irish were yet ready for self-government, and though he disapproved of the savage reprisals that followed the rising in 1798 – the year he was called to the Bar – and smarted under the continual examples of anti-Catholicism, both personal and countrywide, he was not at all reluctant to take his stand against Robert Emmet's rabble when it rose in 1803.

For one thing, though he was still only nominally (if publicly) a Catholic at the time, he could not espouse a cause that was implicitly anti-Catholic and aimed to bring down the Church and its clergy, along with other establishments that Emmet had better reason to execrate. The corruption and injustice that both the United Irishmen and their caudal manifestation in the 1803 rebellion wished to end caused the same visceral response in him, but his head inevitably and sometimes damagingly ruled his heart. His stance was to irritate supporters throughout his long career, notably when Young Ireland found his patronage a drag-anchor. In spite of extreme criticism of him and misunderstanding of his views from such firebrands as John Mitchel, he was just as aware of the power and justice of Emmet's famous speech at his trial as they were and he undoubtedly approved of the aims of his much younger, and impatient, allies. Yet the slightly theatrical asseveration made in a speech on 28 February 1843 in his sixty-ninth year that, 'Not for all the universe contains would I, in the struggle for what I conceive to be my country's cause, consent to the effusion of a single drop of human blood, except my own', was not only sincerely meant but could have been uttered by him with the same conviction at any time during the previous fifty years.

Though called to the Bar on 19 May 1798, three months short of his twenty-third birthday, it was not until the following spring that O'Connell began the gruelling circuitry that was to be the pattern of his life until emancipation opened his career as a parliamentarian. The unrest that was to culminate in the risings had upset the 1798 law calendar and disrupted land communications. His triumphal journey home to Kerry necessitated a thirty-six-hour voyage in a potato boat to Cork, but even though Munster was quiet during the summer and the normal circuit took place, he was too ill to defend cases. This illness – the result of his headlong lifestyle – was a fever characterised by high temperatures and resulting delirium. It was severe enough to leave him near to death; he was so enervated by it that it was nearly Christmas before he could return to Dublin.

It was an odd interlude in the life of a man who until his last years was noted for the relentless robustness of his health. He took to the fatigue and the fretting of circuit journeys as if he enjoyed them. This sense of bodily zest only added to the myth that surrounded him. The vigour, humour and 'play-acting' that characterised his pleading at the Bar and his speeches from the platform increased his stature among his followers. Even if he had remained a lawyer and taken no part in public life, his successes would have won him lasting fame. He could switch from declamation to quippery, from the thunder of the tragedians of the contemporary stage to the risky cheek of today's stand-up comedians. (When he lived in London he spent what time he could at the Haymarket and Drury Lane.) He mocked his opponents with parody and impersonation, yet there was no more dignified or more respectful practitioner before the Bar of His Majesty's courts than Mr O'Connell, when he had the call. He used that summer and autumn in Derrynane as a *reculer pour mieux sauter* and when the spring sessions of 1799 came around he certainly took off.

One of his early successes occurred in that circuit when, instead of waiving his right as junior to cross-examine, he asked a witness at a Tralee court to say just what he meant by the phrase, *'mo chuid uisce beatha'* – 'my share of whiskey' (the word *'cuid* 'in Irish might mean 'little' or 'much') – and put it to him that his share was the whole contents of the tankard 'except the pewter'. The effect was to cause the whole court to laugh heartily and to wring from Jerry Keller, the Father of the Munster circuit, the remark, 'You'll *do*, young gentleman! You'll do!' On another occasion his knowledge of literal Irish and the psychology of Irish witnesses caused an adamant perjurer to collapse under a typical twist in cross-questioning. The case dealt with the signature to a codicil to a will which the witness swore had been made while the testator was still alive; *'Bhí beatha ann'* ('There was life in him'), he kept insisting. Suddenly O'Connell put it to him that he had put a live fly in the dead man's mouth while he held the hand to sign the document. The witness, in tears, admitted everything.

O'Connell needed all his superlative strength and resilient personality to survive the twice-yearly, six-week trudge through the courts of Roscrea, Nenagh, Limerick, Ennis, Tralee,

Macroom, Cork and Cashel, over appalling roads and dangerous mountains passes, for pitifully small fees. He prospered, even though the fatter fees of a senior counsel were denied him and his race and religion remained barriers to him achieving the highest success. Yet by the time he was in his mid-thirties his annual hard-earned income was the modern equivalent of £120,000.

Occasionally his slowly burgeoning political destiny intersected with his legal career. In July 1813 his stirring but ultimately unsuccessful defence of John Magee in the libel case brought by the Duke of Richmond made it clear that the disgraceful partiality of judges and the venality of juries would no longer remain unchallenged. The case, which showed all the traits of his personality, both good and bad, earned him the insignificant hatred of William Saurin (1757–1839), the Attorney-General, and the much more serious enmity of Sir Robert Peel (1788–1850), a hereditary baronet and the new Irish chief secretary. Peel, who though a bitter opponent of emancipation was pragmatic enough to push it through Parliament when there was no alternative, generated an injudicious spleen in O'Connell. He brought out the worst in a man who did not always control his tongue. The inevitable pun 'Orange' Peel had a certain justice since Peel was very much against repeal and was probably anti-Catholic by instinct. Yet to say his smile was like the silver plate on a coffin or to describe him as 'a raw youth squeezed out of the workings of I know not what factory in England, and sent over to Ireland before he had got rid of the foppery of perfumed handkerchiefs and thin shoes' was as close to Billingsgate as one could get.

This contemporary term for low invective came from the 300-year-old reputation for famously ripe language of the porters in the London fish market. O'Connell's facility in it somewhat diminished his reputation in Britain, but his skill in this area was celebrated at home. On one famous occasion he bested Biddy Moriarty, the Ormond Quay stallholder who was the Dublin champion, smothering her with scientific terminology, calling her among other things 'a miserable submultiple of a duplicate ratio' and rendering her speechless with his peroration, 'You porter-swilling similitude of the bisection of a vortex!'

John Magee, of the famous libel case, was a Protestant and the proprietor of the pro-Catholic *Dublin Evening Post*. Peel had arrested him as part of a deliberate policy to harass the liberal press. Already Hugh Fitzpatrick, a Catholic bookseller, had been tried and brilliantly but unsuccessfully defended by O'Connell for printing the 'libellous' book *Statement on the Penal Laws*, by Denys Scully. During the trial the young Turk had had the effrontery to call the famous 'hanging judge', Lord Norbury, and Attorney-General Saurin as witnesses. Now with an even clearer case, the enraged Saurin was determined to make an example not only of the editor but also of the new spokesman for the seditious Catholics. It was the occasion of one of O'Connell's longest and most brilliant speeches, which included a scathing admonition to the all-Protestant jury: ' . . . do not commit, if you can avoid it, this pious crime of violating your solemn oaths, in aid of the pious designs of the Attorney-General against popery'. His conclusion, which in fact proved ineffectual, caused considerable embarrassment in the court-room and confirmed Peel's personal animosity towards O'Connell:

> If amongst you there be cherished one ray of pure religion, if amongst you there glow a single spark of liberty, if I have alarmed religion, or roused the spirit of freedom in one breast amongst you, Mr Magee is safe, and his country is served; but if there is none, if you be slaves and hypocrites, he will await your verdict and despise it.

In fact Mr Magee was not 'safe'; he was found guilty and sentenced the following January to two years' imprisonment with a fine of £500 (about £35,000 in modern terms). By then O'Connell's speech had been published in pamphlet form and his position as the voice of freedom was established. It was only the beginning and it was to be a slow process; the Castle had won that round. None of the newspapers at the time could risk adopting an overtly pro-Catholic, anti-establishment stance.

Perhaps 'The Liberator's Last Case' – as it

might well have been called in the broadsheets – was the most exciting and most typical of his methods. On Saturday 24 October 1829 the 150 defendants arrested for conspiring to kill several landlords in Doneraile, a village about twenty-seven miles from Cork, were tried in three batches in Cork. Four of the first lot were found guilty and sentenced to be hanged within the week, according to the expeditious custom of the country at the time. The friends of those in the second and third batches sent a desperate message to Derrynane that O'Connell might defend the rest. The judge refused to postpone the trial, which went ahead as usual on the Monday. O'Connell, in his fifty-fifth year, had to travel ninety miles of the worst roads in Ireland. Driving himself through the night in a gig with relays of horses and stopping at Macroom for a mere three hours' sleep, he arrived in time for the start of the proceedings. One version of the mythic tale has the last horse drop dead as he alights and stalks into the court, causing John Doherty (1783–1850), the Solicitor-General, to blanch. The word of the paladin's nocturnal dash had got out, and all along the road from Macroom to the city cheering crowds helped him on his way.

O'Connell made short work of his opponent; his objections were upheld by the judges but were somewhat obscured by the bread and milk he was eating as he listened to the briefing from the defence barristers. He tore the suborned witnesses to pieces, totally discrediting their evidence, to the extent that one fellow, visibly trembling, was said to cry out, 'Wisha, thin; God knows 'tis little I thought I'd meet you here today, Counsellor O'Connell. May the Lord save me from you!' The packed jury still had the power to convict, but one honest – and brave – member could not bring himself to give a verdict of guilty on such patently false evidence. The second and third batches were acquitted and the unfortunate members of the first lot had their sentences commuted to transportation. The outcome of the case was the icing on the cake after the success of emancipation and was a suitable curtain call to a most successful first act.

3

ACTS OF UNION

The year 1800 was to prove one of the most significant of O'Connell's whole career since it provided him with the cause that was to dominate his life and also found him the woman who was to be his happily wedded wife. The Act of Union, passed by both parliaments, became law on 1 January 1801, creating the United Kingdom of Great Britain and Ireland. The country was to be represented at Westminster by four bishops, twenty-eight peers and a hundred MPs. This piece of legislation was supported by many Catholics, who believed the promise of Prime Minister William Pitt (1759–1806), mediated through Lord Cornwallis (1738–1805) and Viscount Castlereagh (1769–1822), that full emancipation would follow. When George III found that emancipation was contrary to his coronation oath, he refused to permit further discussion of the matter. Pitt, Castlereagh and Cornwallis resigned but they were soon back in office and it would take nearly thirty more years before full emancipation was achieved, George IV yielding only after the threat of a serious political crisis and the relentless persuasion of the Duke of Wellington (1769–1852) and Peel – men not noted for their liberalism or favourable view of Catholicism.

The young barrister was horrified by the diminution in the political and consequently the moral position of his country. He scorned the alleviatory clauses of the act, thundering in his first public speech at a protest meeting at the Royal Exchange on 13 January 1801 which he helped organise, 'I know that the Catholics of Ireland remember they have a country, and that they would never accept any advantages as a sect that would destroy them as a nation.' He went even further, urging his listeners to join with him in proclaiming, 'that if the alternative were offered to him of union, or the re-enactment of the penal code in all its horrors, that he would prefer without hesitation the latter, as the lesser and more sufferable evil; that he would confide in the justice of his brethren, the Protestants of Ireland, who have already liberated him, than lay his country at the feet of foreigners.'

This was strong stuff, especially coming from a young Kerryman who was unknown outside the Munster circuit. There was no mistaking his forensic ability and the sense that in politics, as in pleading, he would 'do'. Until then Catholic agitation had been in the hands of rich urban merchants and the few Catholic nobles who had been able to hold on to their lands in spite of the anti-popery laws. They were truly a sect, with little interest in national politics and less concern for the ever-increasing population of urban poor and debased tenants-at-will. What they had in common with their poorer brethren was the need to make their way in a country that regarded them as non-citizens, continually humiliated by a corrupt and time-serving ascendancy. Many, including such prelates as Archbishop John Thomas Troy (1739–1823), had supported the Union and were prepared to be ultra-loyal if this would bring amelioration of the condition of Catholics. The champions of the Catholics had in the past included Charles O'Conor, John Curry (c. 1710–80), John Keogh

(1740–1817) and Wolfe Tone, and in true Irish fashion the various Catholic committees were characterised by dissension and a tendency to split.

O'Connell had made it clear that he was prepared to play his part in the movement for Catholic emancipation but, given the glacial pace at which Irish politics progressed, his leadership took some time to become firmly established. His relentless work rate had to be maintained in order to support his wife and growing family. He and Mary had kept their betrothal a strict secret, mainly to avoid the wrath of Hunting Cap, who had already lined up an appropriate wife with an acceptable dowry. He and Mary had met when O'Connell was in Tralee for the summer assizes in 1800, when, discovering that she was fancy-free, he asked with typical dispatch, 'Will you engage yourself to me.' The courtship was mainly epistolary and for most of the time Mary did not complain about the enforced secrecy of the relationship. The fiancé was waiting for an appropriate time to convey the tidings to his irascible guardian. Yet on a sudden urge they persuaded the parish priest of Tralee to officiate at a secret ceremony and they were married on 24 July 1802. Mary soon became pregnant and the hasty marriage could no longer be concealed from Hunting Cap. He was furious and altered his will so that his ward received only a third of the estate; O'Connell did, however, become the owner of Derrynane and was often glad of the house as a retreat and a source income from its rents.

The O'Connells had four surviving sons and three daughters, the eldest, Maurice (1803–53), being born on 27 June at his father's birthplace of Carhen, and, like him, fostered, this time by his O'Connell grandparents. In common with his brothers, Morgan (1804–85), John (1810–58) and Daniel Jnr (1816–97), Maurice became an MP; all four sons were thus beneficiaries of emancipation. Relations between father and sons was usually cordial but his tenderest feelings were for his daughters, Ellen (1805–83), Kate (1807–91) and Betsey (1810–93), who was born in the February of the same year as her brother John. One son, Edward, born in July 1808, lived for only a year. The need to educate and find careers for the sons and dowries for the daughters was to cause a continual strain on O'Connell's finances. His earnings in 1808 were the equivalent of £100,000 in today's currency but throughout most of his life, in spite of the gibes of his enemies, he was in debt. When he died, unquestionably the father of his people, his personal property barely amounted to £1,000 – about £75,000 in modern terms. It was said as a compliment about Pitt that he died poor; the same was certainly true of his Irish adversary.

O'Connell was generous, hospitable and, in keeping with his mythic status as a latter-day Gaelic chieftain, had many dependants outside his immediate family circle. Mary used with justice to complain about the demands made by his endlessly extended family and she had occasion to suggest to him that his dole to a woman with whom he had had a pre-matrimonial affair should not take priority over the needs of his family. He was also notorious for his readiness in standing surety for friends and losing much money when they failed to appear or absconded. The only period when he could briefly relax was when the 'Catholic Rent' in the mid-1820s brought in a steady, unearned income, although most of it went out immediately for the organisation of repeal committees, compensation for tenants who had been victimised by landlords, legal fees, money for books for poor schoolchildren and funds for the Catholic

Association's reading rooms for adults. O'Connell's answer to the charges of using the 'rint' – as the unfunny *Punch* cartoons inevitably called it – for his own purposes was to remind his critics of what his dedication to repeal cost him both physically and monetarily:

> At a period when my minutes counted by the guinea, when my emoluments were limited only by the extent of my physical and waking powers, when my meals were shortened to the narrowest span, and my sleep restricted to the earliest hours before dawn – at that period, and for more than twenty years, there was no day that I did not devote from one to two hours, often much more, to the Catholic cause ... For four years I bore the entire expenses of Catholic agitation.

For many of these twenty years the work was unbearably tedious, as he battled with his warring allies. As R.D., who wrote the entry for the first edition of *The Dictionary of National Biography* (1882), put it: 'It was by quiet unostentatious work of this sort, by framing resolutions for adoption by aggregate meetings, and by unremitting attention to practical details, that in spite of incredible jealousy, he gradually asserted his leadership of the Catholics.'

For many years O'Connell's endless patience and capacity to persuade produced little effect. The continuing war with France kept the economy buoyant and ordinary Irishmen were needed to swell the ranks of the British Army and Navy. In addition, the government assumed emergency powers, suspending habeas corpus and using the Convention Act (1793) to suppress Catholic societies. The dissension within the Catholic Committee was highlighted when in 1808 Henry Grattan (1746–1820) sought to present a petition to Parliament to grant Catholic emancipation, claiming authorisation from the committee to accept the Crown's veto on the appointment of Catholic bishops in Britain and Ireland. The motions were heavily defeated in both Houses, a pattern that was to be repeated until emancipation was forced upon the king by Peel and Wellington.

The veto question continued to split Irish Catholics as petitions were renewed in 1810 and 1813 with Grattan's relief bills. Rome, which was used to this kind of Gallicanism with European monarchies, was prepared to agree. Catholics in Britain, as much in need of relief as those in Ireland, had publicly assented to the veto and were annoyed at the upstart Irish lawyer who was so adamantly opposed to it. The division was along predictable lines: the Catholic aristocracy and most of the rich mercantile class had no objection to George III's formal approval of proposed bishops; the mass of the people and most of the Irish hierarchy were strongly against it. The fault line was almost exactly the same as it had been over the Act of Union but by now it was clear that Union had not benefited Ireland in the least. The dire prophecies of 'A Prospect', the anti-Union squib by Ned Lysaght (1763–1810), were coming true:

Choice turnips shall grow in your Royal Exchange,
And fine cabbages down along Dame Street

and with ominous accuracy:

And well may John Bull, when he's robbed
us of bread,
Call poor Ireland 'the land of potatoes'.

O'Connell's method was to continue doggedly to

advance the Catholic cause, quietly in times of apathy but using grander gestures when the occasion arose. Just as his voice had been heard above those of all other Catholics in his condemnation of the Union in January 1801, now, almost exactly fourteen years later, his fighting words dispelled the fog at a meeting at the Carmelite church in Clarendon Street: 'Let our determination never to assent reach Rome . . . I am sincerely a Catholic but I am not a Papist.' As with many of his gestures, the immediate result of this demand was disappointment. The response of the Holy See was effectively to acquiesce in the veto principle by reassuring the British government that they would appoint only incumbents who were acceptable to the government.

O'Connell's public admission of Catholicism was by then sincere; Mary's epistolary reminders to him when on circuit-court duty of the need for him to observe the rules of fast and abstinence were not longer necessary. Yet he was still enough a man of his time to ignore on one occasion the Church's ban on duelling. On 1 February 1815 across the county line in Kildare, O'Connell answered the challenge of John D'Esterre and mortally wounded him. The cause was apparently trivial: O'Connell had with reason described the Dublin Corporation as 'beggarly' because of its petition against emancipation. D'Esterre, a rather hot-headed – and failing – provision merchant, had chosen to take the blanket condemnation personally and called him out. D'Esterre, as an Orangeman with political ambitions, had probably intended only to humiliate the Catholic champion and show solidarity with Saurin, who was still smarting from his courtroom drubbing. A public horsewhipping would have satisfied him but the matter got out of hand.

O'Connell was gravely shaken and remorseful and vowed never to be provoked to extremes again. Afterwards he always wore a glove on his right hand when he received Communion and offered to do what he could for D'Esterre's widow and children. Yet he was aware that the duel had made it less likely that he would be at the mercy of bullies who would otherwise have challenged him. The seeking of satisfaction was such a part of public life that the enmity between O'Connell and Peel boiled over into the threat of another potentially mortal encounter. The affair fizzled out mainly because of Mary O'Connell's wise manoeuvrings. Ten years later O'Connell apologised publicly to Peel, risking the

DANIEL O'CONNELL

charge that he was 'crouching to the most implacable
and dangerous enemy of the Catholic cause'. The
apology was characteristic of a man whose Catholic
conscience was becoming increasingly sensitive. He
knew his faults better than anyone else and regretted
them bitterly. And so the battle continued, with
O'Connell doing everything he could to raise his
people, often as much against their inclinations as
against their adversaries.

His mien during the visit of George IV in 1821
shortly after his coronation was also literally 'crouching':
he presented a laurel wreath on bended knee to the
bloated king on his departure from Dunleary (which
was thereafter called Kingstown). He also put his
name to a subscription list which was to build a
memorial edifice in memory of the royal visit. This
was another example of O'Connell's royalism, however pitifully inadequate the actual sovereign, and also
of his determination to use every possible means of
advancing his cause. It was due to his years of effort
that the king found it judicious to have representatives
of the Catholic hierarchy presented to him in all their
gorgeous ecclesiastical robes. It was a small advance
but it served its purpose of giving the mass of
Catholics a vestige of pride in themselves.

4

EMANCIPATION

In May 1823 O'Connell formed the Catholic Association with the aim of achieving emancipation as a preliminary to full repeal of the Act of Union. It seemed initially to be another of the combinations that had not been notably successful since Hobart's Relief Act of 1793 removed most of the remaining legal penalties associated with the popery laws. Various other Catholic 'boards' and 'committees' had been formed – and suppressed in 1803, 1811 and 1814 – and this one had no greater hope of survival. Its composition was originally the same as the earlier groupings, consisting of merchants, professional men and landowners, all of whom were vocal and quick to disagree. The association's purpose was final emancipation from confessional disability by 'all such legal and constitutional measures as may be useful'. This meant the recovering by Catholics of the right to be senior government officials, judges, king's counsels, county sheriffs, admirals, generals, cabinet ministers, privy councillors and MPs. There seemed no reason to suppose that, with the continuing disapproval of emancipation from the Castle and the adamantine refusal of the King and his House of Lords to grant it, the association would achieve its purpose.

Yet by the spring of the next year the association had been transformed into the first constitutional political movement with mass population involvement in Europe. The change was effected by the involvement in the process of the majority Catholic population – now approaching a Malthusian danger point of 7 million, many of them the very poor – by the 'penny rent'. At first the membership fee was the customary guinea a year, an unimaginably large sum to the urban and rural poor. O'Connell then put into practice a suggestion made by William Parnell, the grandfather of Charles Stewart Parnell, the 'uncrowned king' of later politics. Anyone could be an associate member of the organisation on the payment of one penny a month. The effect of this measure was remarkable: it not only provided a large annual income for the association but also involved in peaceful protest thousands of people who might otherwise have vented their frustration in agrarian outrage in one of the secret societies that had existed since the formation of the 'Whiteboys' in 1761 or in the slightly less savage faction-fighting.

Though sincerely committed to constitutional means, and loathing and dreading mobocracy, O'Connell was not above an occasional piece of what later ages came to know as 'brinkmanship'. He projected himself as the only one who had the ability to prevent the worst excesses of such bands as the Threshers, the Molly Maguires and the Carders (whose special trick was mutilating people with the spiked steel combs used for carding flax). In the same way nearly sixty years later, in 1881, Parnell was able to warn that if he were to be arrested he would be replaced by Captain Moonlight. Agrarian violence did diminish after 1824 and 'Orange' Peel not only had to admit that this was due to the benign influence of the association but suffered the additional embarrassment as Home Secretary of having the Orange Order suppressed under the Unlawful Societies Act of March 1825. The Catholic Association was suppressed under the same act but a new version which kept itself 'o' th' windy side of the law' was in place by August, its position made secure by one of the subtlest lawyers in Ireland.

The activities of the association were not only political but also pastoral and educational. It was an agency of adult education and in this regard was second only to the *Nation* (1842–8) newspaper and the Gaelic League in the first twenty years of its existence. The second O'Connellite stroke was the politicisation, for better or worse, of the Irish clergy, whose power and dignity he had done so much to affirm in the doldrum two-score years after it was created. Ex officio members of the association, they became his agents and the trainers of a network of politically mature voters. The appointment in each parish of two churchwardens – one chosen by the priests, the other by election by the laity – established at a stroke local agencies to do the varied work of the association: collecting the rent, countering the proselytising of the evangelical agencies, compensating evicted tenants, especially those who voted against their landlord's nominees, arbitrating in land disputes, maintaining the association's reading rooms with their free newspapers and doing what they could to stamp out secret societies. The establishment of five inspectors per county under a national inspector laid the basis for what the British authorities dreaded: a kind of alternative, Catholic government.

The association's politicisation of what had been an illiterate and debased underclass laid the foundation for a hundred years of mainly constitutional agitation for Irish independence. It supplied Parnell and later Redmond with as effective a parliamentary team and as supportive an electorate as Westminster was ever to experience. The republican tradition – as exemplified by the hotter heads among the Young Irelanders, the Fenians and the combined Citizens Army and the Volunteers who rose in 1916 – was maintained by a tiny minority until the Anglo-Irish War of 1919–20, and even then the

IRA could not claim to have the entire nationalist
population behind it. O'Connell dreaded the
possible effects of armed uprising, not so much
on the perceived enemy as on the Irish themselves. His unabashed shade might still be a
formidable opponent in a debate about the
Ireland of today.

The success of the Catholic Association in
both its terms – 1823–5 and 1825–9 – established
O'Connell, who had hitherto been no more than
a well-known member of the Catholic lobby, as
what Balzac called the incarnation of a whole
people. He was a flawed hero who made many
mistakes, sometimes because of mistrust and otherwise because of being too trusting. He was not a
great originator and his knowledge of his country
and its past was instinctive rather than precise. Yet
his flair for persuasion, for effective rhetoric, for
inspiration of his people and for organisation were
remarkable. Any good tactic that was presented to
him was efficiently developed and made successful
now that his organisation effectively covered most
of Leinster and Munster.

This was most obvious in the defeat of Lord
George Beresford in Waterford in the general

election of 1826. The idea had come from Thomas Wyse (1791–1862), a Catholic merchant who with the help of the local parish priest organised the Catholic voters, many of them Beresford's tenants, to vote for Henry Villiers Stuart (1803–74), a liberal, pro-emancipation Protestant. The Beresfords, a notably anti-Catholic family, essentially owned Waterford, and in those days before the Ballot Act of 1872 it took courage for the forty-shilling freeholders, as those at the lowest level of franchise were known, to vote against their Ascendancy masters. Once O'Connell understood the possibilities of the move he swung all the resources of his association behind Villers Stuart. The voters were marshalled and the usual pattern of drunken rioting was avoided. O'Connell toured the county making speeches for the opposition candidate and was by his side on the polling days. Elections, held then normally every seven years, were leisurely affairs and there was time for the same kind of success in Louth, Monaghan and West-meath. The Catholic Rent enabled the local officers to compensate those who were victimised by their landlords.

Daniel O'Connell
(National Library of Ireland)

O'Connell's home in Derrynane, County Kerry
(National Library of Ireland)

A monster Repeal meeting held at Tara in 'Repeal Year', 1843:
Note the banners carried by trade unions, the use of images of
harps, wolfhounds and round towers and the enthroned Irish
harper in the centre of the picture

(Mansell Collection/Time Inc/Katz Pictures)

NOTICE.

WHEREAS, there has appeared, under the Signatures of "E. B. Sugden, C., Donoughmore, Eliot, F. Blackburne, E. Blakeney, Fred. Shaw, T. B. C. Smith," a paper being, or purporting to be, a PROCLAMATION, drawn up in very loose and inaccurate terms, and manifestly misrepresenting known facts; the objects of which appear to be, to prevent the PUBLIC MEETING, intended to be held TO-MORROW, the 8th instant, at CLONTARF, *to petition Parliament* for the REPEAL of the baleful and destructive measure of the LEGISLATIVE UNION.

AND WHEREAS, such Proclamation has not appeared until *late in the Afternoon of this Saturday, the 7th*, so that it is utterly impossible that the knowledge of its existence could be communicated in the usual Official Channels, or by the Post, in time to have its contents known to the Persons intending to meet at CLONTARF, for the purpose of Petitioning, as aforesaid, whereby ill-disposed Persons may have an opportunity, under cover of said Proclamation, to provoke Breaches of the Peace, or to commit Violence on Persons intending to proceed peaceably and legally to the said Meeting.

WE, therefore, the COMMITTEE of the LOYAL NATIONAL REPEAL ASSOCIATION, do most earnestly request and entreat, that all well-disposed persons will, IMMEDIATELY on receiving this intimation, repair to their own dwellings, and not place themselves in peril of any collision, or of receiving any ill-treatment whatsoever.

And We do further inform all such persons, that without yielding in any thing to the unfounded allegations in said alleged Proclamation, we deem it prudent and wise, and above all things humane, to DECLARE that said

Meeting is abandoned, and is not to be held.

Signed by Order,

DANIEL O'CONNELL,

Chairman of the Committee.

T. M. RAY, Secretary.

Saturday, 7th October, 1843.
3 o'Clock P. M.

RESOLVED—That the above Cautionary Notice be immediately transmitted by Express to the Very Reverend and Reverend Gentlemen who signed the Requisition for the CLONTARF MEETING, and to all adjacent Districts, SO AS TO PREVENT the influx of Persons coming to the intended Meeting.

GOD SAVE THE QUEEN.

Browne, Printer, 56, Nassau-street.

The notice, signed by O'Connell, calling off the monster Repeal meeting planned for Clontarf

(National Library of Ireland)

There was great jubilation for it was realised that in seven years' time unionist members would be thrown out in most Irish constituencies. This was, however, a long time to wait and the living conditions of many of the association's supporters had not improved. The population was too great for the land system to support and the landlords were, in general, as irresponsible as ever. In 1828 the member for Clare, William Vesey Fitzgerald, was made President of the Board of Trade, and according to the parliamentary procedure of the time he had to stand for re-election. He was a resident landlord who was pro-Catholic and popular with his tenants and had held the seat for ten years. A suitable rival Protestant candidate was sought but when no obvious candidate emerged O'Connell accepted the idea that he should stand himself. Though prevented by law from sitting as a member, there was no legal reason why he should not stand.

His campaign was fierce but heavily supported by donations from all over the country. He made much of the anti-Catholic nature of the oath that any MP had to take and acted the stage Irishman in his cajoling of the crowds at his election meetings. The small farmers, eerily well-disciplined and marched by their clergy to the hustings, supported him to a man. He defeated his opponent by 2,057 votes to 982 and with a kind of irritating naivety apologised to Fitzgerald for the robustness of his tactics. Euphoria gripped Catholic Ireland and rose to dangerously high levels; O'Connell believed – or let it be known that he believed – that if the people were frustrated again he might not be able to control them. Wellington, as Prime Minister, and Peel, as Home Secretary, realised that emancipation had now to be granted and thought to use one of O'Connell's earlier concessions to nullify its practical effects, at least in the short term. The basis of his power – the courageous, if volatile, forty-shilling free-holders – was disenfranchised; the minimum qualification was made a valuation of £10 and the number of voters outside the boroughs was reduced by 87 per cent to 37,000. Things improved after the Great Reform Bill of 1832, and after the greater enfranchisement in 1868 the anti-Union Irish MPs became a significant element in parliamentary politics.

What had been granted by the 'Act for the relief of His Majesty's Roman Catholic subjects' of 13 April 1829 was potential rather than actual since most of the significant posts were still reserved for Protestants – indeed unionists. Michael O'Loghlen (1789–1842), the first Catholic law-officer for two centuries, was not appointed Attorney-General until 1835 – and afterwards became the first Catholic judge. The very prospects of papist relief inflamed Orangeism, which always had many more supporters in Ascendancy Dublin than in Belfast, and, as Brunswickism, involved many of the administration in the Castle. In areas like Counties Antrim, Down and Armagh, where membership was demotic, there was a real danger of a recrudescence of the eighteenth-century violence between latter-day 'Peep o' Day Boys' and 'Defenders', now called 'Ribbonmen' and facing a somewhat-less-tolerated Orange Order. The act might be described as the Treaty of 1921 was by Michael Collins as offering 'the freedom to achieve freedom' – and it was reacted to similarly by some separatist critics. The attenuated nature of the relief it seemed to offer, combined with Wellington's dark words about the state of Ireland and his threat to resign, finally moved the King to sign the act.

It was a mighty victory and the country rejoiced – but followed O'Connell's typical and wise instructions that any celebrations should stay this side of exuberance. O'Connell's friends realised that a parliamentary career meant a drastic cutting down of his legal earnings and the expense of a London establishment. He was given a testimonial of £30,000 and from 1830 a yearly pension, which amounted to £13,000 at times and became known as the 'tribute', providing his enemies with the easy gibe of calling him the 'big beggarman'. Given the temperament of the pensioner and the need he had for that kind of steady income, he might well have called himself, in the words of a Dublin street song of the time, the '*jolly* beggarman'.

With a lack of grace that has always seemed to be a characteristic of British politicians, especially Tories, in their dealing with the Irish, the government inflicted one last humiliation on the man who not only in Ireland but throughout the world was now known as the 'Liberator'. He had already been excluded from the list of Catholics called to the Inner Bar (on the instructions, he believed, of Peel, though the latter blamed the King) in October 1829 – the most successful lawyer in Ireland not fit to be made a KC! – and now, because his election in Clare had taken place before the passing of the emancipation act, he was required to resubmit himself to the electorate. Before going to the country he went to the Commons, read through the oath of allegiance with its offensive anti-Catholicism and refused to swear it. He was returned unopposed after a triumphal entry into Ennis accompanied by 40,000 followers and many bands and banners. This piece of Tory spite had prevented his becoming the first Catholic to sit in Parliament since the reign of James II; a number of English Catholics had already taken their seats and the Duke of Norfolk was admitted to the House of Lords.

5

TARA – AND CLONTARF

When O'Connell, described by Yeats as the Great Comedian, in deprecating contrast to the, to him, more acceptable 'tragedian' Parnell, belatedly took his seat in the House in November 1829 he was in his fifty-fifth year, still vigorous but showing the signs of the inevitable maiming and grime that involvement in Irish politics entailed. In a letter to his financial secretary, Patrick Vincent Fitzpatrick (1792–1865), on 14 May 1839 he wrote:

> I will never get half credit enough for carrying Emancipation, because posterity never can believe the species of animals with which I had to carry on my warfare with the common enemy. It

is crawling slaves like them that prevent
our being a nation.

The strain of being genial, courtly and funny
needed the relief of the odd splenetic outburst.
The lies or economies with the truth that he
found it necessary to utter to carry out his
mission of re-creating the Irish race did not
please him and it was something of a release to
be courted by the Whig administration as an
ally. Repeal was his ultimate goal and if he
suggested to his sorely tried followers that it was
almost within his grasp, this was as venial as
assuring his audiences at monster meetings that
the Irish mountains were the highest in the
world. Repeal was not to be had from even the
Whig party, and for the Tories to release Ireland
would have sent an unwelcome message to the
builders of what was to be the great British
Empire. The 1832 Reform Act provided him
with about thirty repeal MPs, and he used these
to help the Whigs defeat Peel's government in
1835 and wrest a series of undramatic but highly
significant reforms from the government for the
period of the Whig administration.

The agreement with Lord Melbourne (1779–1848) and Lord John Russell (1792–1878) was known as the Lichfield House compact; it was informal and was described by Russell as 'an alliance on honourable terms of mutual cooperation'. To some later commentators the 1830s was a period of inertia and too great an amount of 'honour' in dealing with the Whigs. O'Connell had had apparently inert decades before and the reforms he brought about, often with the cooperation of the enlightened under-secretary Thomas Drummond (1797–1840), were in practice much more to the advantage of the Irish than was emancipation.

Drummond had attained notoriety on his appointment in 1835 by reminding and shocking the landowning class – which now included many Catholics – that 'property had its duties as well as rights'. His rationalisation of tithe payments as rent charges in 1836 did much to end the vicious 'night' war that for four years had caused many deaths and much agricultural damage and maiming of farm animals. The same year he replaced the local (and often partial) constabularies with a disciplined central force, the Irish Constabulary, and in the capital created the Dublin Municipal Police, a model of what an unarmed civilian peacekeeping watch should be. His pressure on local Orange magistrates and his rigorous policing led to the salutary if temporary dissolution of the Orange Order. Catholics were appointed to all levels of government service, most significantly to the posts of Solicitor- and Attorney-General. Municipal reform led to O'Connell being elected Lord Mayor of Dublin in 1841; he was the first Catholic since 1690 to fill the post. There were urban Poor Law reforms but the state of the rural poor was still dire.

The reforms may seem to later ages tame but if ever a man knew that politics was the art of the possible it was O'Connell. He worked within his own set parameters, and if that frustrated Young Ireland – the next generation of reformers, who were already knocking at the door – it was simply a sign of a different interpretation of the *Zeitgeist*. Meanwhile his avuncular wooing of the young Victoria was perfectly in keeping with his Grattan- esque vision of the 'King, Lords and Commons of Ireland'. Her accession in 1837 after at least eighty years of anti-Catholic, reactionary Hanoverian

rule gave the easily cheered-up Kerryman renewed
hope, though this was dissipated when the light-
hearted Regency princess came under the influence
of her consort, the Protestant (and truly Victorian)
Albert of Saxe-Coburg.

The fall of Melbourne's Whig administration
in 1841 relieved O'Connell of the need to acquiesce
in the Lichfield House policy. His old adversary
Peel, the new Prime Minister, had by now
somewhat mellowed in his attitudes to Catholicism
and Ireland and was showing the genuine, if
glacial, integrity that has caused modern historians
to regard him as second only to Gladstone among
nineteenth-century British statesmen. One cannot
help engaging in the vain speculation as to how
the history of Ireland might have been altered if
the destructive enmity between O'Connell and
Peel had not persisted. It would have given time
for the old warrior to accept, say, the office of
Master of the Rolls which the Whigs would have
granted him, and he might have spent his last
years in judicial dignity, unquestionably like his
hero George Washington, the 'father of his country'.
However, his beloved Mary had died in 1836 and
he lost not only a wife but an unusually sound

counsellor. He felt that she would have urged him to carry on the fight and not desert his people. A Repeal Association, which had been formed in 1840, brought in much more money than the Catholic Rent. It also introduced O'Connell to new and not always welcome allies.

Thomas Davis (1814–45), the posthumous son of an English army surgeon and a Mallow Protestant, discovered in himself, while at Trinity, a deep sense of Irish nationality. A man of messianic zeal but a poor speaker, he joined with two Catholics, Charles Gavan Duffy (1816–1903), a journalist from Cavan, and John Blake Dillon (1814–66), from Roscommon and, like Davis, a lawyer. In October 1842 they founded the *Nation*, a weekly repeal paper, with the purpose of educating the Irish in their history and culture and reassuring them that nationalism was now as much the property of Protestants as of O'Connell's *canaille*. They published news items, essays and stirring ballads – much of the material written by Davis – that would in the words of one of his most famous efforts make Ireland 'a nation once again'. Davis also urged his readers to save Irish as a native language before it was lost. *The Spirit of the Nation* (1843), a collection of the paper's verse, was for many years the most popular Irish anthology; it went into at least fifty-three editions and was still in print in 1934.

One of the ballads, Davis's 'Orange and Green Will Carry the Day', to be sung to the tune of 'The Protestant Boys', was an index of Davis's understanding of the need to come to terms with the island's other tradition. O'Connell, like many other nationalist leaders since, never seemed to sense the true temper of the Ulster majority. His one foray into Belfast – in 1841, to sell repeal – was unsuccessful, his anti-Union arguments easily refuted by Henry Cooke (1788–1868), the founder of the Presbyterian General Assembly: 'Look at . . . Belfast and be a Repealer if you can!' The prosperity of at least the east of Ulster, where a kind of appliqué industrial revolution artificially created by Britain was taking place, was clear proof that for a majority of northern Protestants the Union was working. The different system of land tenure there, too, meant that even Catholic tenants had more rights in the North than in the South. The Ulster question was a matter for many another day and the land question was to be settled long before repeal.

Free from the need for loyalty to the Whigs and with a sense of renewed vigour, O'Connell used his old technique of involvement of the ordinary people in his agitation. In 1843 he held a total of thirty-one mass meetings in such centres as Limerick, Kells, Charleville, Cork, Cashel, Nenagh and Mullaghmast, the numbers steadily increasing until the culmination at Tara on 15 August, when he gathered 750,000 to hear his vocally relayed oratory. It was Thomas Barnes, the hostile editor of the London *Times,* who named them 'monster' meetings – the Frankenstein reference fully intended. In the organisation of these hostings the younger men, now known as Young Ireland, in an imprecise analogy with Mazzini's *Giovine Italia* (1831), worked vigorously. Their (limited) acceptability to Protestant liberals filled a gap in the repeal platform but members like John Mitchel and Thomas Francis Meagher (1822–67) were already distant voices prophesying war.

The climax of Repeal Year was to be the meeting at Clontarf on Sunday 8 October 1843.

Like Cashel and Tara, the venue was chosen because of its association with a glorious Irish past. The meeting was, according to the publicity, going to make the Tara host look 'like a caucus'. On the Saturday evening, when many protesters would have started for the capital, Peel proscribed the meeting. Already warships rode at anchor in Dublin Bay and Clontarf was ringed with cavalry. O'Connell immediately cancelled the meeting, with the agreement of the Young Irelanders, although they afterwards denied this. O'Connell's decision was entirely consistent with his lifelong policy of non-violence: the prospect of nearly a million people converging on the fields and strands of the bay, to be met by armed and trained soldiers, was unthinkable. He organised stewards to turn back the crowds that were already converging on the city and was present on the ground at Clontarf, standing in front of the detachments of riflemen and dragoons to shoo away any who thought to defy the proclamation.

Peel helped save O'Connell's political reputation by having him, his son John and seven other prominent repealers arrested on a charge of 'unlawful and seditious opposition'. Repeal now had several prominent martyrs, and Dublin Castle reacted atavistically by having a totally Protestant jury, which at the trial in May 1844 found the accused guilty. O'Connell was sentenced to a year's imprisonment, fined £1,000 and bound over for seven years. His sojourn in the Richmond Bridewell was, personal liberty aside, anything but penal. The governor's house was put at his disposal and daily visits from many friends and clients were not prevented; visiting the prison became a recognised social event in the capital that summer. An appeal was lodged with the House of Lords, where on 4 September, of the five Law Lords, three Whigs, opposed by two Tories, overturned the verdict. The Liberator, as he was now universally known, was drawn home through the streets of Dublin in a gorgeously decorated triumphal chariot, surely pleasing his love of glitter. It was his last hour of triumph.

6

GENOA AND ROME

Soon after his release a great mental and physical change was observed in O'Connell. He showed more and more symptoms of the illness which would end his remarkable strength and mental application. The cause was probably an abcess in the brain which would develop into the meningitis which killed him. This may well have been a side effect of surgery he had undergone for piles two years before. It showed itself in deterioration of his handwriting and occasional lack of concentration. His condition did not affect his will or other mental processes but he tired easily and perhaps his judgement was not as sound as it might have been a decade ago. He also embarrassed his family and friends by becoming infatuated with a young Belfast woman called Rose McDowell (c. 1821–1902), the daughter of a liberal Presbyterian merchant. McDowell moved in repeal circles and had visited O'Connell in gaol. She was probably flattered by the attentions of the most famous man in Ireland and without Mary's steadying hand he seems to have assumed that his feelings were reciprocated and asked her to marry him.

Peel now made a number of reform suggestions which might have been welcomed had they come from Russell; instead they were interpreted, perhaps correctly, as attempts to win away moderate Catholic support from the now more extreme agitation of the repealers. Peel proposed that the Maynooth grant be tripled to £26,360 and made permanent, that charitable bequests be administered by a new board that would have Catholic members, that three secular Queen's Colleges be established in Belfast, Cork and Galway and that a commission look into the vexed question of landholdings. O'Connell welcomed the first suggestion but owed too much to the repeal support of John MacHale (1791–1881), the archbishop of Tuam, to deal with the charities and colleges questions fairly. Three Catholic bishops had already accepted positions on the charities board when other members of the hierarchy, led by MacHale, condemned it.

The question of the colleges, which were specifically secular so that Catholics might attend them without any sense of confessional commitment, received even greater reprobation, MacHale insisting that Catholics could not attend lectures in such godless institutions on history, logic, metaphysics, geology and even anatomy. To hear lectures from non-Catholics on such inflammatory topics would place their 'faith in imminent danger'. It did not say much for the strength of the belief of the educated Catholic laity if it could not stand up to such temptations, but MacHale, like O'Connell, was very much a man of his time and preferred ignorance to risk. When as a response to the education question the Irish hierarchy established the Catholic University in 1854, MacHale disapproved of the appointment of John Henry Newman (1801–90), partly because he was English. The O'Connell of earlier decades would not have disapproved of the idea of non-denominational colleges but now his clerical allies were no longer convenient pawns.

The Devon Commission, though composed mainly of landlords (causing O'Connell to remark,

'You might as well consult butchers about keeping Lent'), did a remarkably thorough job and its submissions would have slightly improved conditions between landlord and tenant – there was even a suggestion of compensation for improvements – but that the landlord-packed House of Lords predictably blocked it. The education question showed clearly the divergence between Young Ireland and O'Connellism. Davis in particular was personally hurt by O'Connell's stance. After his death from scarlet fever in 1845, the more extreme elements among his companions were in the ascendant. The rejection by them in 1843 of the federalist ideas put forward by a number of liberal Ulster Protestants, led by Sharman Crawford (1781–1861), as a compromise between Union and repeal, after O'Connell had publicly approved them, had already caused dissension. O'Connell's old affirmation on non-violence, which was now sounding almost parrot-like, proved too much for Duffy, Dillon and the rest. Young Ireland formally seceded from the Repeal Association in 1846: the Liberator had brushed the burrs from his coat.

By now the cataclysm of the potato failure was

to render most politicking irrelevant. The partial failure of the crop in 1845 had been dealt with fairly effectively by Peel, who allocated £100,000 to buy stores of Indian corn to prevent absolute starvation, provided £365,000 to subsidise the funds of the local relief authorities and split his party by abolishing the protectionist Corn Laws. Blight ruined the harvest again in 1846 and the true nature of the catastrophe became clear as the death toll from starvation and typhus soared. O'Connell's last speech in the House, made at the peak of the Hunger in February 1847, was painful to friends and foes alike. The great actor's voice was gone: the man whom many thousands believed spoke for them at his mass meetings was barely audible. The only words that the Hansard reporters could catch were:

> Ireland is your hands . . . your power. If you do not save her she cannot save herself . . . I predict . . . that one fourth of her population will perish unless you come to her relief.

His grisly prediction was only too accurate; Ireland's population of 8.2 million (according to the 1841 census) was diminished by death and forced emigration by more than 2 million.

Daniel O'Connell set out on a last journey to Rome at the beginning of March and had reached Genoa by painful stages, although he was in physical and mental turmoil by the middle of May. He died there after two days of relative peace on the evening of 15 May. His heart was, on his instruction, placed in a shrine and taken to Rome by his chaplain, Dr Miley, and his fourth son, Daniel. It was placed in the Irish College at Santa Agata dei Goti; his body was taken home to Dublin, thus providing many generations of Irish schoolchildren with the mantra 'My soul to heaven, my heart to Rome, my body to Ireland.' Folklore has it that as the *Duchess of Kent,* carrying the corpse, was sailing up the Liffey, it was passed by the emigrant ship *Birmingham,* loaded with desperate emigrants fleeing the Famine, and that their keen for the dead leader was loudest of all. The body was laid to rest in Glasnevin in the 'Great Comedian's tomb', now under a round tower, 165 feet high, erected in 1869 and aesthetically true to its time, as was its incumbent.

One of the remarks attributed to O'Connell in

1846 was: 'I will not be six months in my grave when the flag of rebellion will be unfurled in Ireland.' In 1848 William Smith O'Brien (1803–64), the Young Irelander who had led the Catholic Association while the Liberator was in Richmond, reluctantly put himself at the head of a rebellion that amounted to little more than a skirmish at the Widow McCormick's garden in Ballingarry, County Tipperary, on 29 July. This incident finished Young Ireland, whose members were subsequently imprisoned or deported. Their historians did not actually blame O'Connell for its failure but their account of their four-year alliance is biased against him to the point of libel. The Ballingarry caper was not significant at the time but it helped suggest to later apologists that the tradition of resort to arms had been continuous since 1798. The Fenian founder James Stephens (1824–1901) had been out with O'Brien and it was an old Fenian, Tom Clarke (1858–1916), who came to Dublin in 1907 to revive the Irish Republican Brotherhood and plan the Easter Rising.

O'Connell's insistence on constitutional methods was unlikely to appeal to a country that achieved freedom for three of its provinces by force of arms. His amenability, friendliness even with his adversaries and toadying to royalty all seemed hateful to the austere and often puritanical members of republican groups. Mitchel's splenetic description of him in his *Jail Journal* (1854) – 'Wonderful, mighty, jovial and mean old man. With silver tongue and smile of witchery and heart of melting truth. Lying tongue, smile of treachery, heart of unfathomable fraud! What a royal yet vulgar soul!' – seems now oddly complimentary and demonstrates, if nothing else, what a psychological gulf there was between the Dungiven Presbyterian and the Kerry chieftain. His posturing, purposive vulgarity and his general merriment offended as well, and the remark made when he was twenty-one still causes smart: 'The Irish are not yet sufficiently enlightened to bear the sun of Freedom. Freedom would soon dwindle into licentiousness; they would rob, they would murder. The liberty which I look for is that which would increase the happiness of mankind.' It is idle but tempting to wonder what his comments would be about the condition of his beloved country and the people he raised from wretchedness now, a century and a half after his death.

SELECT BIBLIOGRAPHY

Doherty, J. E. & Hickey, D. J. *A Chronology of Irish History since 1500*. Dublin, 1989.

Edwards, R. D. *Daniel O'Connell and His World*. London, 1975.

Foster, R. F. *Modern Ireland, 1600–1972*. London, 1988.

Kee, R. *The Green Flag*. London, 1972.

MacDonagh, O. *The Emancipist: Daniel O'Connell, 1830–1847*. London, 1989.

MacDonagh, O. *The Hereditary Bondsman: Daniel O'Connell, 1775–1829*. London, 1988.

Moley, R. *Daniel O'Connell: Nationalism without Violence*. New York, 1974.

Moody, T. W. & Martin, F. X., eds. *The Course of Irish History*. Cork, 1994.

O'Faolain, S. *King of the Beggars*. London, 1938.